OPERATION
CES SUCCESS

Operation CES Success

By Mike Lizun, Matt McLoughlin, and Alfred Poor

Copyright © 2016 by Gregory FCA

June 2016

ISBN 978-0-9826526-9-5

Published by:
Desktop Wings Inc.
700 East Walnut Street
Perkasie, PA 18944
215-453-9312
www.desktopwings.com

OPERATION
CES SUCCESS

by
Mike Lizun,
Matt McLoughlin,
and
Alfred Poor

Acknowledgements

Everyone here at Gregory FCA would like to acknowledge the many technology clients we have helped through the years to make their CES experiences successful. Without your faith and commitment, we never could have mastered the art of CES success!

Dedication

This book is dedicated to the professionals at Gregory FCA and their tireless commitment to their clients in the practice of public relations. You never cease to amaze us all with your knowledge, expertise, hard work, and results!

Foreword

CES can be a scary place.

I know this firsthand. For more than a decade, I've been working with the CTA (previously the CEA) to produce conferences and events within the framework of CES, shining light on new technologies for lifestyle applications. Our "Living in Digital Times" programs cover everything from children to seniors, from health to higher education.

We also created the popular "Last Gadget Standing" and "Mobile Apps Showdown" competitions that play to standing-room-only crowds at CES every year.

Over the years, I've had the opportunity to work with hundreds and hundreds of technology companies of all sizes, from international giants like Samsung to tiny startups that go without sleep for the week leading up to CES in hopes of getting their prototype to work reliably, or maybe even work at all.

I've witnessed the meteoric rise of new companies, launched by their appearance at CES. Fitbit and Misfit both began their lives at CES with tiny little booths that grabbed the public's imagination. Car manufacturers like Ford and BMW basically reinvented their companies for a digital age right on the CES show floor.

On the other hand, I've seen companies show up and then never be heard from again. Having a compelling story and knowing your objectives before you set foot on the Strip are paramount.

There are no guarantees in business or in life. It's fitting that CES takes place in Las Vegas, as it's a high-stakes game where the rewards can be life-changing.

While you can't guarantee that you'll win, you can do your best to nudge the odds in your favor. And one of the best ways to tilt the table to your side is to learn from what others have done before you.

In the following pages, you will benefit from the authors' different perspectives as well as their decades of combined experience.

What I like best about this book is that it focuses on practical information that you can put to use right away, no matter what your circumstances. Is your company big enough to float a six-figure investment in a CES campaign? They have you covered. But what if you need to scrape by on a shoestring budget? They have solid advice for you as well.

Sure, it would be great to spend 18 months preparing for CES, and this book shows you how to make the most of that. But even if you need to create a crash program with only a few months' lead time, you can make that work, too.

It's all in here, from initial planning to preparation, from execution to follow up. And along the way, you'll learn all sorts of insider tricks and strategies to maximize your return on investment, to stretch your budget dollars further, and to not just survive but to enjoy and to grow from the experience.

I wish all the companies I work with at CES could have had a guide like this when they were starting out. Even CES veterans would likely benefit from reading this.

In short, this book will make CES a much less scary place, and will help you make the most of your investment of time, money, and people when you choose to exhibit at the show.

Along with the authors, I wish you great success at CES.

Robin Raskin
Founder and President
Living in Digital Times
www.livingindigitaltimes.com

Contents

Acknowledgements iv

Dedication v

Foreword vii

Introduction: What Are You Thinking? 1

Chapter 1: Step One – Answer the "Why"s 5

Chapter 2: Planning – Too Early Is Almost Early Enough 13

Chapter 3: How to Plan a Standout PR Campaign 27

Chapter 4: The Big Enchilada – the Booth 43

Chapter 5: The Un-Booth – Alternatives to Booth Exhibits 53

Chapter 6: Las Vegas Survivor Secrets 65

Chapter 7: Go It Alone or Get Help? 77

Chapter 8: Make the Most of Your Investment 85

Summary: Lather, Rinse, Repeat 93

About the Authors 99

About Gregory FCA 101

Introduction:
What Are You Thinking?

There comes a time for any technology company – small or large, startup or established – when the people in charge have to confront the age-old question: "Should we go to Las Vegas and exhibit at CES?"

Officially, it is the "International Consumer Electronics Show," and since 1967, it has been the most significant technology show in the United States. The main show is held in January in Las Vegas, but the Consumer Technology Association (CTA) holds related events throughout the year and around the world.

In 2016, more than 3,800 companies chose to exhibit at this

show in Las Vegas, where they covered more than 2.47 million square feet of exhibition space. More than 170,000 industry professionals came to see what they had to show.

In short, it's a big show. A really big show.

So you think maybe it's time for your company to jump in and take a spot in this enormous circus. You might want to heed this famous quote's advice about physical exercise:

> *Whenever I get the urge to exercise, I lie down until the feeling passes away.*

[Often attributed to Mark Twain, the original source was likely Paul Terry of the Terrytoons animated cartoon fame.]

If you lie down and the feeling does not pass away, then read on. On the following pages, you will find years of experience boiled down into a comprehensive and accessible crash course in how to succeed at CES.

We have relied not just on our own experiences, but on the combined wisdom of exhibitors and the technology press who have covered them over the years. In this book, we give you detailed information about what to do – and what not to do – to make the most out of the time, money, and other resources that you must dedicate to a successful CES campaign.

The fact is that many companies have made great gains by exhibiting at CES: large and small, startups and going concerns. Whether you seek investors, distributors, technology partners, press buzz, or something else, the effort spent on a campaign in Las Vegas can deliver an enormous return.

We will take you step by step through the whole process, and help you develop a practical plan that will give you the best chance of success.

And we hope to see you at CES next January!

All I'm saying is you could've told me this is not so much a cosplay thing.

EXHIBITS

CES

Blazek

Chapter 1:
Step One – Answer the "Why"s

"If you don't know where you're going, you might wind up someplace else."

A presence at CES can catapult a company into the public spotlight, or it can be a colossal waste of time and money. One of the most important factors in determining the impact of your presence is whether or not you have clear goals.

Before you can begin your planning, before you can consider questions of staffing and publicity and booth size, before you can map out the hundreds of small and large decisions, you must make one key decision: Why are you going?

This question gets at a basic issue: How are you going to judge whether or not your efforts were a success? What do you hope to accomplish?

There is no one right answer to this question. It all depends on where your company is in its growth. It depends on your product or service, and its stage of development. Here are four common reasons that companies want to exhibit at CES:

Sales

To some readers, this may seem trivially obvious. Why wouldn't you want sales? Isn't that the only reason for being at CES?

It's certainly true that you may be able to fill your order book at CES. A huge number of distributors, wholesalers, corporate buyers, and individual retailers attend the show, and they are certainly looking to buy. According to the CTA, 83% of the "top retailers" were represented among the attendees at CES 2015.

If your product or service is ready for the market, then racking up sales can be a good goal. If your product is launching at CES (or you hope to launch soon after), then you still may want to focus on booking some advance sales. One company executive told us that 70% of their entire year's sales to distributors and retailers came directly from contact at the show.

But there are other good reasons to exhibit at CES beyond just selling your product or service.

Make a Media Splash

Another common goal is to gain visibility for your company.
For some, it's the hope of hitting it big, much like coming
up with a YouTube video that goes viral. That sort of
publicity can take your company from zero to sixty so
fast you'll risk whiplash.

But even if you don't become the talk of the show, getting
some buzz within your market can be priceless. Let's face
it: Editorial coverage costs you nothing compared to paid
advertising space that gets your message across. And as one
media advisor told us, your presence at CES can have an
impact on how your company is talked about in the press
for an entire year.

We don't know of any specific technique that is guaranteed
to make a big media splash, but there is a lot you can do to
increase your odds of getting more coverage before, during,
and after the show. (We cover specific strategies for this goal
in depth in Chapter 3.)

Find Funding

You can get money to fill your company's bank account in
ways other than selling your product or services. Venture
capitalists and other investors are roaming the halls trying to
sniff out the next Big Thing in technology. And they have fat
checkbooks that they are willing to open for the right prospect.

For example, Eureka Park is a special exhibit space that caters
specifically to startups and small companies. According to

the CTA, these exhibitors have raised more than $1 billion in investments since 2012.

One famous example of these companies is Indiegogo, which, after first exhibiting in Eureka Park, raised more than $56 million in three years. Another example is Pono Music, a company founded by music legend Neil Young to provide high fidelity digital music. The company exhibited in Eureka Park in 2015, and went on to raise more than $12 million. Owlet Baby Care exhibited in Eureka Park in 2015 and 2016, and has raised about $9 million in funding.

In fact, the CTA maintains a Top 100 Leaderboard of companies that have exhibited at Eureka Park, and all of the companies on the list have raised at least $1 million in funding.

Meet Potential Partners

If you have a small company – especially if you're just starting out – it can be very helpful to have a big friend in the playground to help look after your interests.

You might need partners to help with production. Many new companies follow a "fab-less" model in which they contract out the manufacturing of the actual product, made to their design specifications, rather than build and maintain their own manufacturing facility. You will find lots of representatives for such companies at CES, as they look for new clients for their services.

You may also be able to establish partnership arrangements

with larger companies that are above or below you in the supply chain. If your product relies on specific parts or materials, you may be able to make cooperative arrangements with a company that can supply them for you.

On the other hand, your technology may form the basis of a larger product or service offered by other companies. They may be interested in forming a partnership to create a closer relationship between your two organizations.

CES is the setting for all sorts of partnership deals, and can be an excellent opportunity to meet with the executives who can make this happen.

Success by the Numbers

These goals are not mutually exclusive, but you definitely want to prioritize them so that you don't try to do everything at once.

The best way to sort through all these choices is to come up with some specific goals for your CES experience. Wherever possible, quantify the goals so that you can measure your performance against your expectations. When you have measurable goals, you can be much more objective about whether you were able to achieve them or not.

For example, a goal might be "Within four weeks after CES, we will have $250,000 in product orders."

Or "By the end of February, we will have closed at least $250,000 in new funding to bring our prototype into production."

As an added bonus, consider making a low, middle, and high goal. The low number is the minimum acceptable return on your investment. The middle number is a good result that will make you and your colleagues happy. The high number is the "grand slam" level that exceeds your wildest hopes.

Once you know what exactly you are chasing after, you'll be in a much better position to make your plans. Your specific goals will help you make the hard choices – large and small – as you prepare for success at CES.

Action Guide: CES Goals

Rank the four goal categories 1 through 4 in order of their importance:

Sales   Media coverage   Investors   Industry partners

_____   _____   _____   _____

For each goal, include measures if possible, including quantities, deadlines, or dollar amounts.

Top priority:

_____

_____

_____

_____

_____

Secondary priority:

_____

_____

_____

_____

_____

Listen, just get set up. We'll argue later whether it was a good idea to try to get a booth at the last moment.

BOOTH #869

Blazek

Chapter 2:
Planning – Too Early Is
Almost Early Enough

"The early bird gets the worm," and that's certainly true for CES. The earlier you can start planning, the better prepared you and your team will be. You will have the time to consider all the possibilities, and will have plans in place to deal with any contingencies.

An early start also means that you're more likely to get the booth that you want. You'll be able to save money every step of the way through early discounts or by avoiding rush orders.

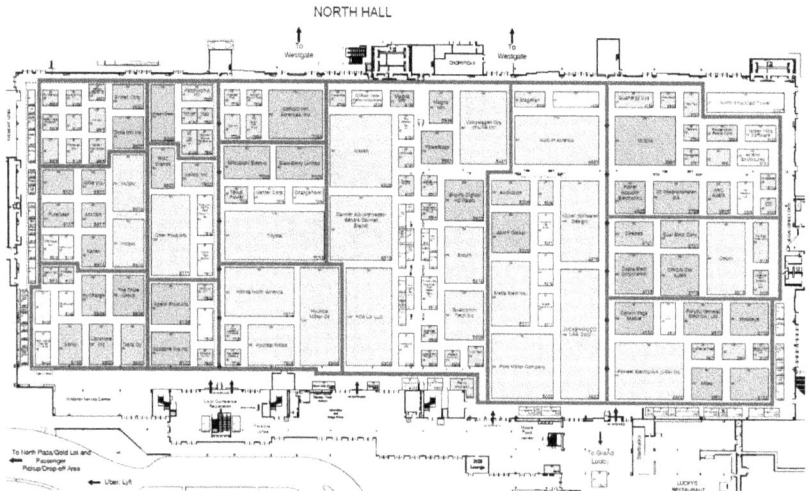

But don't be afraid to decide at the last minute to just go for it. It's not the optimum choice in most cases, but some companies can make it work.

Let's start with the long-range approach first.

How Soon Is Too Soon?

Ideally, you want to start at least a year in advance to plan your debut at CES. There are many good reasons for this, but the most important one is that this will give you a chance to go to the show and look at it through the eyes of a potential exhibitor.

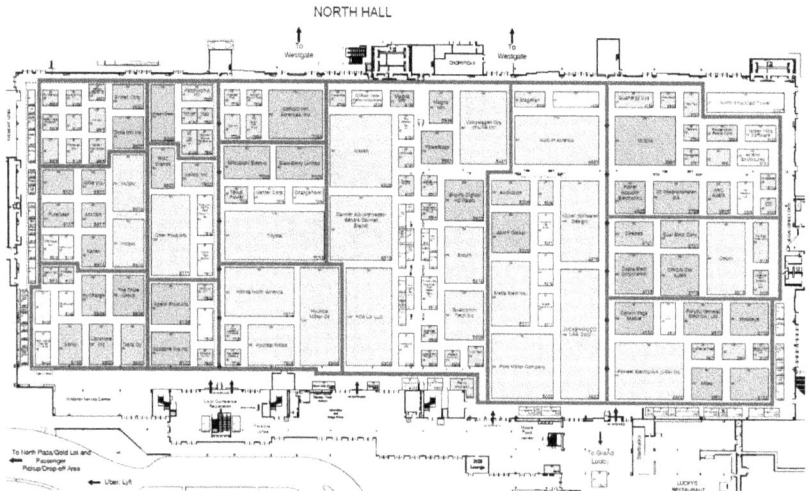

The Las Vegas Convention Center (LVCC) North Hall is the place to find automotive and high-end audio exhibitors. (Credit: CTA)

Visit all the halls, and scope out who else in your industry is exhibiting, and where. Visitors will go to certain areas to find products for a given market, so you want to be where they will find you. For example, the North Hall shown above is the place where you'll find automotive exhibits as well as many of the high-end audio exhibits. The Sands Expo, shown below, is home to wearable technology, health and fitness products, 3D printing, and home automation.

Sands Expo, Level 2, Halls A-D

Wearables, health and fitness, 3D printing, and home automation are found at the Sands Expo. (Credit: CTA)

Study other booths, from the big-production extravaganzas of the multi-national mega-corporations to the 10-by-10 booths of the small companies and startups. What works, and what doesn't? Look for ideas that you can use to save money and still make a big impact.

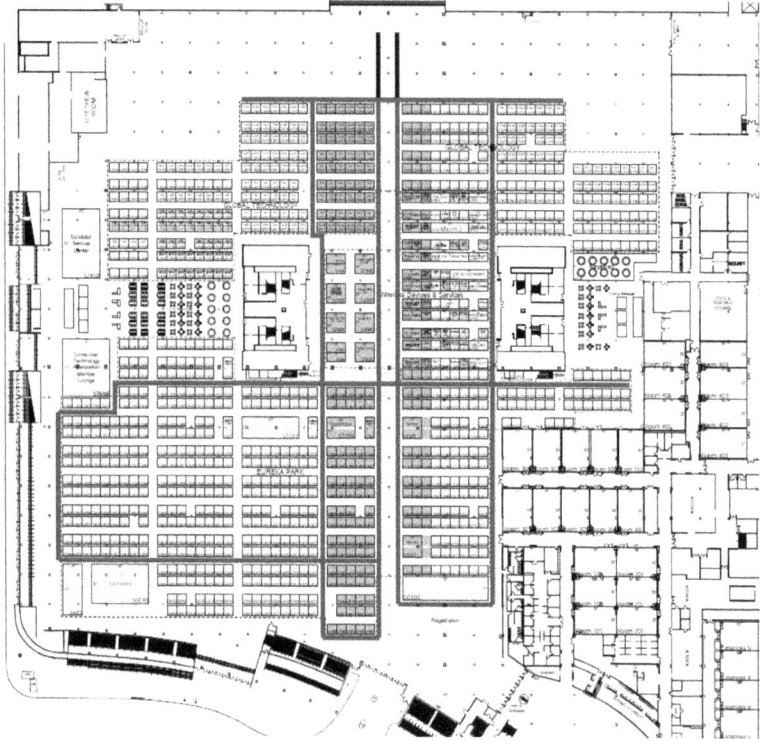

Eureka Park provides smaller exhibit spaces at a lower cost for qualifying exhibitors. (Credit: CTA)

Be sure to check out the low-rent districts in the exhibit halls, including Eureka Park, where many startups and university projects have displays. The location and configuration of Eureka Park – pictured above – changes from year to year; most recently, it has been a growing part of the Sands Expo exhibits.

Note that companies must qualify in order to exhibit in Eureka Park and take advantage of lower rates. The exhibit spaces are crammed together and it can be more difficult to be found, but it does offer a lower-cost option. Take the time to meet the CTA representatives, and find out the details about your options for exhibiting at next year's show. As we heard from other companies, the exhibitor materials can be confusing and even misleading. You get a seemingly endless stack of contracts, instructions, and optional services for everything from carpet to electricity. There are all sorts of rules and restrictions about what you can and cannot do.

You may find it easier to get your questions answered by speaking directly with a CES sales representative so that you reach a clear understanding of what you get (and don't get) for your exhibit fee, and how you can comply with all the other requirements. Contact information is available on the CES website in the Exhibitor section.

Sharpen Your Pencil

Once you have the information that you need about the show, it's time to get serious about budgeting for the event. There are many costs to consider, and the more you can account for them in advance, the fewer problems you'll have when crunch time comes (and it will come, no matter how well you plan.)

You have two main resources at your disposal: money and staff time. You must consider both; if you don't have enough of both to apply to the project, you can end up wasting all of it.

Show Me the Money

The money is probably the easiest part. You will need to rent your exhibit space (or not, as we'll cover later in this book), but that's just the tip of the iceberg. The cost for your booth will vary by its location and size, and your choice will depend largely on what you can afford and what impression you want to make. For 2017, for example, the standard booth rental is $43 per square foot. The minimum 10-by-10 booth is 100 square feet, so the starting point is $4,300. (If you qualify for Eureka Park, the booth fee could be much lower.)

If you have ever exhibited at a trade show of any size, you know that everything is extra. Here are some examples from the exhibitor materials for 2017: While there is no charge for handling packages that weigh 50 pounds or less, you'll pay $45 to $100 to have your materials delivered to your booth; electricity will cost from $85 to more than $550, depending on your needs and when you place your order; labor to install and dismantle your booth, or to hang your signs, or handle electrical services will cost $75 to $95 an hour (plus more for overtime); and your booth fee does not even include carpet, so figure on a minimum of $110 for a 10-by-10 booth, with better carpet costing $270 to $300 plus another $63 for padding.

You can outfit your entire booth with rental furniture and accessories. A 6-foot table will cost you $56, $80 if you want it draped. A table lamp rents for $135, and a wastebasket is $10. These are the discounted prices if you order online; add about 10% if you order later.

Be sure to find out what all this will cost in advance. If you're new to this game, be prepared for some sticker shock; you can often purchase an item for less than it costs to rent one. You're paying for the convenience of having the items delivered to your booth space, and if necessary, installed for you. (And as we'll discuss later, there are obstacles in the way of you providing some of these items for yourself.)

You also need to budget for any items that you'll include in your booth. You may have costs for signage, display furniture, and equipment that you'll need to display or demonstrate your product or service. You may want to provide tables and chairs where your staff can sit and talk with prospective customers.

If your product relies on a wireless connection such as Wi-Fi, and you plan to demonstrate it, know that the service can be problematic in the exhibit halls. As you might expect, there will be enormous competition for the airwaves, so even if you sign up for Wi-Fi service, it may not function well. Consider other ways to demonstrate your product if possible. For example, the graphics processor company NVIDIA configured stand-alone servers that contained the company website and other related content. It was able to access this over a wired connection instead of arranging for live internet access, which gave it a stable and fast demonstration platform that it controlled.

NVIDIA brought its own servers so it could access its own content without having to rely on internet service at the show.

There are other direct costs to consider. How are you going to disseminate your information? Depending on your target audience and your goals, you may want to hand out printed literature. (Note that many company representatives and members of the press pointed out that most of the printed handouts end up going to the recyclers.)

You may want to store the information digitally, and either hand out cards with links to the data, or hand out copies of the data itself. If you want to give out copies of the data, your best choice is a USB stick. (See the next chapter on how to keep the press happy.)

Another out-of-pocket expense will be the travel costs for your staff. Unless you're planning a team-building road trip, you'll probably have airfare as a budget item. You'll also have to consider ground transportation, accommodation, and meals for your staff, plus any entertainment expense you might want to spring for as a reward for surviving the week. (We'll get into some tips and tricks for making your dollars go further in Chapter 6.)

In talking with other companies about their first-time CES experiences, we were told that you can get by on a shoestring for as little as about $10,000, or you can spend $100,000 or more (and even much more)! Don't put your business in jeopardy by over-spending, but don't scrimp where it will reduce your visibility and your chances of being noticed.

Frank McGillin of Neurometrix, a wearable technology firm, advises companies to be "ruthless" about controlling the budget, as it is easy for spending to quickly spiral out of control. Examine each expense under the microscope of "What is the incremental impact of this item?" If it isn't likely to provide a strong return on investment, give serious consideration to cutting that item.

It's All About People

As much as you may spend in cash on a CES campaign, you will spend much more on your human resources.

The most obvious cost is staffing your booth. Assuming that your team is small, you will probably have everyone show up to set up and prepare the booth, stay in Las Vegas the whole time, and then head home again after breaking down the exhibit. That's eight to 10 consecutive days per person. If they work the typical 50 weeks a year, this amounts to 4% of their entire work year. If you take into account that CES days are typically 12 to 14 hours long, you'll have to budget for overtime pay as well.

Make sure that you pick staff who are outgoing, friendly, and approachable. You don't want people who hang around in the back of the booth, chatting with each other and staring at their smartphones. You need people who are going to proactively engage with visitors. If you don't have these people on staff, or can't spare this much time for them to be away from their normal duties, consider hiring some temp workers whom you can train to help out in the booth.

But wait, there's more. Someone has to design the booth, arrange for the rental of the booth and all the other details, schedule the travel, find lodging, make sure there's plenty of bottled water in the booth at all times, and a hundred other time-consuming details. Either you're going to outsource some of these tasks (increasing your dollar budget) or you're going to have to pull one or more staff members off their normal duties – possibly for several weeks – to take care of all this.

And then there's the question of what is going to happen in the booth. You can anticipate press, investors, industry partners, retailers, wholesalers, distributors, and just plain curious civilians stopping by your booth. What are you going to say to them, and who is going to say it?

A big part of your planning tasks will be to achieve clarity on your message to the different audiences, and then develop appropriate responses. What will you say to attract people into your booth? What will you ask to help identify (and qualify) them? Who will be responsible for taking the discussion to the next level, whether it's technical, sales, marketing, or financial?

Once you have this worked out, you need to spend time training your staff. They need to know how to respond to different situations. They need to be able to provide satisfactory answers when they are not the ones qualified to deal with that topic. There is absolutely nothing worse than a prospect stepping into a booth and being told, "I'm sorry, there's nobody here who can talk to you. Maybe you can come back another time."

The bottom line here is that you can easily spend a few days to a week per person on your team, developing your message and then rehearsing so that it comes out smoothly.

And when you get back, you'll have an unusually large number of contacts with whom you'll need to follow up. (You'll find more on this in Chapter 9.) This can clog your business development channels, especially if they need to be handled by one specific individual, such as a C-level exec who leads all financial negotiations. Have a plan in place to handle potential bottlenecks at this stage in the process.

Taken all together, you can add another 2% to 4% to your staff's time for preparation and follow-up, for a total of 6% to 8% of their total work year. What would happen to your business if you sent these people on an extra four weeks of paid vacation? How would their work get done? That's the question you will have to answer when you're working out your staffing budget for your CES campaign.

Speak the Language

One final note on staff costs: If your company is short on native English speakers, you may want to consider hiring some temporary workers who can handle the first level of greeting and categorize visitors. This will increase your dollar budget, but can make your campaign much more effective. One place to find these people is through any U.S.-based partners, who may have people who can help out. You can also go through temporary staffing agencies to arrange for booth greeters. If you have a public relations firm helping you, they may also be able to source temporary workers for you.

Kow is Director and co-founder of Well Being Digital Ltd. (WBD101), a technology design house in Hong Kong that develops health and fitness products. From the first time that he exhibited at CES, he realized the importance of staffing the booth with "native English speakers" in order to engage visitors more effectively.

At the same time, if you anticipate meeting potential partners or investors from other countries, such as in Asia or Europe, be sure to have someone who is fluent in their language, or better yet, is a native speaker. If necessary, hire a translator who can bridge the communication gap. That will go a long way toward lowering resistance and making your communication more effective.

Action Guide: Budget

What will your CES campaign cost you? This list of items is not comprehensive, but instead is to get you thinking about the direct and hidden costs that will be required.

Dollar Budget:

Item	Amount
Booth fee	$_____
Carpet and fixture rental	$_____
Electricity	$_____
Internet	$_____
Booth display materials	$_____
Equipment for booth	$_____
Printed materials	$_____
Digital materials	$_____
Shipping (to and from)	$_____
Staff travel (airfare)	$_____
Ground transportation	$_____
Lodging	$_____
Meals, snacks	$_____
Entertainment	$_____
Other: _____	$_____
Other: _____	$_____

Staff Budget:

Item	Staff	Days per staff
Booth setup		
Staffing the booth		
Booth teardown		
Travel		
Logistics planning		
Message development		
Message rehearsal		
Post-show follow up		
Other: _____		
Other: _____		

Boy, just when you thought you've seen everything at CES.

CHARGING EEL

Blazek

Chapter 3:
How to Plan a Standout
PR Campaign

The talk of CES 2016 was a two-year-old Chinese startup named EHang that makes drones.

Leading up to the show, the company had built a lot of momentum; a year earlier, its first product, the Ghost Drone, hit 784% of its goal in an Indiegogo campaign. Ghost Drone 2.0, released later in 2015, let users control the drone through a VR headset. In the company's first 16 months of existence, it raised more than $50 million.

But at CES, drones are literally everywhere. To stand out, EHang needed a product that was different from what everyone else would be showing, a drone that would instantly capture the attention of media – and their audiences.

You probably saw what they came up with. It was featured on CNN, CNBC, Wired, TechCrunch, Fortune, Entrepreneur, NPR, Popular Science, Digital Trends, and other top-tier outlets.

The EHang 184 is a drone large enough to carry a single person in a cockpit, navigating based on a location entered on a smartphone app. It's like a personal, four-rotator helicopter, except you don't need to have any idea how to fly. Just enter your destination in the app and it'll take you there.

How did EHang attract the attention of not only the tech media, but the business and major media as well? And how can you win the same for your standout product? There are a few tried-and-true CES strategies that have gotten dozens of companies like EHang the press coverage they deserve.

Why Media Relations Is a Winning Strategy

Will Rogers once said:

> *Get someone else to blow your horn and the sound will carry twice as far.*

The point is that news about your product or service will carry much more weight if you can get a third-party to say it for you. Not to mention that editorial coverage is free, which is a whole lot cheaper – and often more effective – than buying ad space either in print or online. A story that gets picked up by the press can result in coverage worth hundreds of thousands of dollars. CES is a great place to make that happen.

There has long been a difference of opinion about media coverage at CES, and you might hear some argue that with so much competition, some companies can never generate exposure. That's not our experience. We'd bet EHang would also beg to differ.

What we've found is that this is the one time of year that technology reporters are ready to cover cool products. Even among nearly 4,000 exhibitors, there are ways to stand out and get noticed. The key is how you strategize and connect with the media.

How to Get a Response from Media (Hint: Act Like a Real Person)

Emailing your press release to every name on the CES media list is a losing strategy we call "spray and pray." Instead, work the problem from the other direction. Find articles on websites and in trade journals about your industry and your competitors. Note who wrote those articles. Ideally, you can try to cross-match them with the CES press list, but you can also reach out to them directly.

Start by mentioning something relevant that they have written. "I saw your article about [product], and thought you might be interested in our new offering. We'll be at CES in January, and would love to schedule a time for you to come by the booth. Or we can provide you with information now if you want to include us in any pre-show coverage."

This approach tells them that you respect their time enough to at least find out what they write about, and to bring them some relevant information. It shows that you're making an effort, and not just carpet bombing the press with your message.

In addition to the individuals who write relevant articles, find the contact information for the editor of the publication if you can. If it's a larger organization, they may be sending multiple people to the show, and can direct your lead to the person who will be covering your topic.

Before the Show: How to Arrive in Vegas Ready to Wow the Media

We encourage clients to begin CES planning months ahead of time, often in late summer or early fall, to fully leverage every opportunity come show time. That planning includes determining what products to announce, story themes to develop, events to attend or sponsor, and story angles that appeal to specific media points.

CES is a madhouse, but it's the largest aggregation of technology media under one roof. A well-planned campaign that is thoughtfully integrated with line show introductions is the best way to assure your news is noticed and covered by the media. Here's how to do it:

Build out your product pipeline to peak at CES.
The press attends CES for news, and if you have nothing new, playing the media game is all the more difficult.

Start as soon as possible to create a pipeline of products and new features that will hit in time for CES.

Know that for most media, simply announcing a product is not interesting. Your story has to have some valid and unique angle to it. "Firsts" are always a good sell. When French startup Kolibree debuted the world's first smart electric toothbrush at CES in 2014, everyone from USA Today to Forbes to CNET to NPR took notice. Using Bluetooth and your smartphone, it can tell you how long you spend brushing your teeth and how well you're doing. It used familiar technology (sensors, Bluetooth) in an entirely new context that caught many reporters' attention.

One word of caution: Be careful about stretching to reach a superlative claim, such as a "first." If you have to over-qualify your story – "the first left-handed, solar-powered, vanilla-flavored toothbrush" – reporters may give you the brush off. And if it turns out that your product is not first, or fastest, or lowest priced, or whatever your claim might be, you risk losing credibility with the press.

When at all possible, use numbers to tell your story. A device that's 10 times faster or costs half as much is much more meaningful than one that's simply "faster" or "less expensive." When Faraday Future rolled out its much-hyped FFZERO1 concept car at CES 2016, it touted the 1,000 horsepower electric engine, 0-60 time of under 3 seconds, and top speed of over 200 miles per hour.

As you introduce your new products, don't use jargon. Explain your product in terms an eighth grade student can understand; if reporters need more technical details, they'll

31

ask for them.

Accept the timing and do your homework. Media relations is near-impossible the first full week of January. Most media are out of pocket over the holidays, which makes for chaos that first week back. The fix? Start seeding media early in December to schedule interviews and demos during the show.

Keep an eye out for media leaving tidbits over their social channels of what they're looking for, where they're going, and how to reach them. Jon Swartz of USA Today specifically posts who from his team will be attending the show.

"I'll go on Facebook or Twitter, and I will say, 'Look, here is our team that's going to this event. Here are the four people, and here's what each of us is going to cover or try to cover,'" Swartz noted in a recent interview. "It gives people an idea of what's going to interest us at a show."

Watch for that post and understand what each reporter is looking for: a feature, an op-ed, a review? Target your outreach accordingly.

Register for pre-show media events. Pepcom, ShowStoppers, and CES Unveiled never fail to win media coverage. They come with additional fees, but they also provide exclusive media access that the larger show cannot provide. Most of the companies that get major coverage out of CES are at these shows.

In 2015, the Belty smart belt made its debut at CES Unveiled. The wearable, a product of French startup Emiota, loosens and tightens automatically as the wearer's waist size changes, whether from sitting down or eating a large meal.

The media loved it. By debuting the product at Unveiled, two days before the show started in earnest, Belty rose above the noise and became the talk of CES. Articles in CNET, The Verge, and Gizmodo hit first, followed by stories on CNBC and Yahoo Tech, all before CES even began. On the first full day of the show, Belty was in USA Today. The momentum spread to further coverage on CBS News, Engadget, Cult of Mac, and others, not just during the show, but in the weeks after as well. It might not have had the same success if it had skipped the pre-show events and stayed tucked away at its booth on the show floor.

Craft your news release and other assets. That's right, a news release. A well-crafted story, complete with stats, facts, and details, can help win coverage because you made it easier for the press to report.

Don't forget B-roll, product shots, and fact sheets either. They sound so old school. But in the rush to cover so much news, media want information that can be easily referenced. As one reporter said, "I can always ignore too much information, but it's difficult to make up information that I don't have."

But forget thumb drives and don't even think about printed sheets or CDs. For most media, a link to all the files will do just fine. Current editorial cycles move at the speed of light, so just make sure everything is easy to find and fast to download. Put the link on a business card just for the press, and remember to include the links in any pre-show or follow-up emails with press contacts. Be sure to have the story fully baked and ready to go, regardless of how you deliver it.

DON'T blast your press release to every reporter on the media list. This is worth noting a second time. Too many companies (and PR firms) simply spray and pray. The truly successful, however, pitch with the precision of a surgeon. They know who will be there, what they're interested in, and why this particular product will matter to them. Quality over quantity.

You are much better off sending a personalized and targeted message to 100 good contacts than you are blasting off 2,000 emails to people who will never cover your story. It takes more time and effort to identify the right people, but it can be far more effective in the long run.

Look beyond the typical media. There are a number of outlets that might be interested in running a piece about your company and your plans to exhibit at CES that might not immediately come to mind:

» Your industry association's website, newsletter, or magazine

» Your local newspaper

» Your local television station

» Your local radio station (especially if they have a business show)

» A regional magazine

» A regional business journal

Many of these don't have the resources to send a staff member – or even a freelancer – to the show, so you can offer to provide coverage of the show for them, with a story about the products that got a lot of buzz (including yours, of course).

You can provide content in other forms as well. For example, pitch your local TV or radio stations with an exclusive, live interview from the show floor, either by phone or video chat using Skype or some other service. Don't just report on your product, but include news about the coolest and most interesting products you've seen.

You can also offer to provide an interview segment before or after the show. Bring in four or five products – including your own – and demo them on the air with the hosts. TV loves visual products, especially when they are high tech.

Many local media outlets, including newspapers, will do round-up pieces about local companies that are showing at CES. Reach out to them to see who will be working on the story, and if they don't have one planned, offer to help them with contacts at other companies in the area.

Also reach out to bloggers and podcast hosts who cover your industry or related topics. Any advance coverage provides "social proof" to other reporters and news outlets that you have a story worth covering. And you can refer to this coverage when you contact other press outlets to build and grow a story.

Depending on your industry, consider reaching out to other media outlets for specific audiences. For example, women's magazines are interested in stories about health, diet, weight loss, and beauty. If your product or service falls into any of these categories, reach out to the editor and see if your product would fit into a round-up story. Note that some of these magazines plan their editorial calendar months in advance, so you'll want to make your initial contact in August or September if possible.

At the Show: The Guerilla Guide to Attracting Top-Tier Reporters

You've paid handsomely for a booth on the floor. Maybe you're in a highly trafficked area, maybe you're outside the main action of the show. Either way, getting media to come by your booth to get a firsthand look at your product and talk with your staff should be your goal. There are five major ways to do so.

Set an appointment. The best way is to get a reporter to commit to a booth appointment. Understand that they are inundated with such requests, so only extend the offer to those most likely to be interested in what you have to say.

It helps if you've already got some buzz going (such as through the pre-show events that we'll cover in more depth in Chapter 5); this can generate walk-ins from the press, so be prepared to handle these as well.

After the visit, be sure to get the reporter's contact information and make a note of any follow up details they requested. Do they want an editorial loaner so they can evaluate your product? Do they need a copy of test results or research that was mentioned during the interview? Do they need any special information **right away** because they are going to file their story before they go to bed?

Staff up your booth. Know who is prepared to speak to reporters, and make sure that one of these people is always available in the booth to handle this task.

One veteran reporter told the story of being promised an interview with the CEO at a new company's booth. When he arrived, he was told the CEO was stuck in traffic from the airport, but would be there soon. The clock ran out, and the reporter made and confirmed a replacement appointment for the next morning. When he showed up, the CEO still was not there, and no one else was available to speak with him. Thirty minutes later, the reporter had to leave for his next appointment, and is not likely to cover this company in the future.

Work the floor. Unless you're Samsung, Panasonic, Nikon, or one of the other tech behemoths, you likely won't have a booth in a premier location. So, if you want media attention, you have to get moving. Here are some ways to get started:

» Patrol the expo entrance for media arriving at the hall. It's easy to be overwhelmed by the hundreds of booths. Help them decide where to start.

» Become allies. Do any neighboring booths have products in common with yours? Attract media with a trend instead of a single product. Share these leads with the press; tell them where there's a hot story at your ally's booth. If it's on target for their coverage area, they'll remember you.

» Know what's new. When CES introduced Tech West, a mecca for up-and-coming tech companies in fitness and health, wearables, food tech, 3D printing, robotics, pet tech, and more, CNET staked out the area with its own booth, where exhibitors could pitch their products via tablet to earn a "First Look" video session on CNET.com.

ABD: Always Be Demoing: EHang's person-carrying drone separated it from competitors. But if you don't have an eye-catching new product, you can still get creative and go beyond the typical in-booth display and demo.

In 2015, IO Hawk chased after media with its segway/motorized skateboards, BleachBright offered free teeth whitening, PowerDot showed how attendees could supplement their nightly workouts with mobile-app-controlled muscle stimulation, and we walked the show floor wearing our client's red-light hair growth helmet.

But be sure you're ready to go as soon as media approach your booth. In 2016, we came across a booth with some interesting-looking speakers. After chatting with an exec from the company for a few minutes, he was nice enough to demo the product. Or at least he tried.

Each of the 30 Wi-Fi-enabled speakers in the booth had its own network. When the exec opened his phone settings to select the Wi-Fi for the speaker he was showing, he had difficulty remembering which network belonged to which speaker.

Hey, stuff will go wrong. Luckily, we weren't reporters or important buyers. Always triple check that you and the tech are ready when your number is called.

Be the media and create photo ops. Sometimes the first day of the show is slow outside of Central Hall. Make the most of that time by breaking out your smartphone and snapping some photos, then post and tag to social, like the media would. Go live from the show floor – interview someone from the product team about what they're demoing, what they're seeing at the show, and what trends they're following.

Use interesting visuals to attract media. The media knows that the best way to bring CES to consumers is to show them cool stuff, and many simply want to take a good photo or video and run with it. If you exhibit your product in a visually engaging way, have a device that's unique – or wacky or weird – and you're attending one of the CES pre-shows, there's a good chance you'll capture the media's attention early.

After the Show: CES Is Just the Beginning

Be sure to follow up with any media promptly if you owe them any materials or information, especially if it is going to be part of their show coverage. Many outlets won't cover a story that's a day old and stale. (Others might cover it as much as a week later, which is why it pays to know your contacts and their work.)

If there isn't a need to send information immediately, give them a few days to get settled, and then send a follow up email to check in. Thank them for taking the time to visit the booth, and offer again to provide any additional information they might need.

For many exhibitors, CES is equally about scoring publicity at the event, when technology coverage is at its apex, as well as meeting and creating relationships with media for future opportunities. CES offers the rare chance to open a direct conversation with the media, but it's up to you to keep the dialogue going over the weeks and months afterward.

When coverage goes live, post and repost. The media moves in packs. If others are reporting your story, they feel more comfortable doing the same, especially when deadlines are tight and there's space and time to fill.

Also, members of the press now live and die based on page views, whether they are on staff or freelance. If you help promote their articles and bring them new readers, many will notice and appreciate the effort. And they will be more likely to cover your products again in the future.

A Friend in the Playground

Mounting a successful PR campaign at CES involves a lot of moving parts. From finding the right contacts to making an effective pitch to managing the booth experience, it's a lot to get right the first time.

In many cases, you can get an enormous return on a small investment simply by making your campaign more efficient and effective. This is one reason (of many) that you might want to consider outsourcing some or all of the tasks.

If you can find a PR firm with experience in your market segment, you can piggyback off its existing relationships with the press, analysts, and influencers.

Not only can this save you time, but it can greatly increase your chances of success.

Action Guide: Public Relations and Press

Here's a checklist of items you should consider when preparing your press campaign for CES:

☐ Identify reporters who write about your market.

☐ Come up with an attractive angle for your story.

☐ Prepare a digital press kit to hand out in the booth.

☐ Contact reporters individually by email to offer a booth appointment.

☐ Be sure to have someone in your booth at all times who is prepared to speak with the press.

☐ Follow up on requests for more information immediately.

☐ Contact reporters within three to five days after the show to offer any follow up materials.

☐ Do not ask to be notified if they publish any stories about your company.

It's either Virtual Reality or Modern Dance. I'm not sure yet.

Blazek

Chapter 4:
The Big Enchilada – the Booth

It's easy to be intimidated by the exhibits of other companies.

At CES, you will see mountains built out of large high-definition televisions. You will see celebrities making pitches for a company's products. You will see multi-level booths complete with meeting rooms and private lounges. Some big corporations spend more on the design and construction of their booth than the entire annual budget of many small companies.

Bottom line: Don't feel as though you have to keep up with the Joneses on this one.

Having said that, your booth does make a difference. A single folding table and some chairs are not going to grab the attention of passers-by, nor will they tell the story of your company or its products (at least, it won't in any positive way). How do you decide what to do with your space?

Part of the decision process is a question of what you can afford. Basically, there are two strategies. One is to spend as little as possible. The other approach is to make it look as though your company is much bigger than it really is. Both strategies have their merits.

Make Do with the Minimum

If you want to limit your expense as much as possible, you'll get a 10-by-10 booth space. This will limit where you'll be located; you likely will be relegated to the outer edges of the main exhibit halls, or the low-rent rabbit warren that is the Eureka Zone.

You also don't know who your neighbors will be. CES participants are primed to find multiple booths for similar products in the same general area. If you are off in Siberia somewhere, surrounded by other companies that have nothing to do with your market, your chances of being found by accident are greatly reduced.

Still, a low-cost, small booth can be extremely effective. If you visit CES the year before your first exhibit, keep an eye out for small booths that draw a crowd. They are the exception rather than the rule, but they are proof that you can make a splash even with the smallest booth.

Go Big or Go Home

The other approach is to roll the dice and play with the big boys. This increases the financial risk, but it can yield big payoffs.

WiseWear is a new company that has a product line of smart jewelry that tracks physical activity, links to your smartphone to provide notifications, and can trigger a distress message in an emergency. And when the company first exhibited at CES, it had precisely 10 people in the entire company.

It picked a double-sized (10-by-20 foot) booth on a corner, right on the front edge of the wearable technology section at the Sands Convention Center. It was a tiny new company, but it was rubbing elbows with segment giants such as Fitbit and Withings on the show floor.

In part due to its location, it got far more foot traffic in the booth than it had hoped to get. And the crowded booth attracted more people, including press, and it ended up getting an enormous amount of media coverage at the show.

The WiseWear story was covered by USA Today, The Today Show, Fast Company, Mashable, and Engadget ... and that was just on the first day! This was a "zero to 60" success; it had no press coverage at all before the start of the show.

Basic Principles

Whether you go big or small, the fundamentals of your booth design remain the same.

The most important mission of your booth is to tell a story about your product or service. It needs to be told as quickly and directly as possible, because visitors make snap decisions about whether they will take the time to visit a given booth.

One of the common complaints we hear from members of the CES press corps is that when they approach a booth, they often don't have any idea what the company does. Putting your company name up in giant glowing letters does not do much good if it's not familiar already. This is especially true if the name is some clever, but unpronounceable, combination of consonants that don't mean anything.

You have about three to five seconds to grab a person's attention and for them to decide whether or not your product is relevant to their area of interest. You need to make a clear and bold statement about what your business is, and why you have something worth a second look.

Beyond telling the story of your product to grab a visitor's attention, you also want to be careful about what your booth says about your company. If you have a few poster board signs propped up on tables, people are going to assume that you have some university project with no budget. On the other hand, if you have a cohesive and coordinated design, that can signal a professional operation.

Your signage needs to address the needs of three different types of readers. Develop it based on what we call the "3-30-3 Rule." The idea is that some people will spend three seconds looking at your booth signs, some will spend 30 seconds, and some will spend 3 minutes. You want to be sure that you have content that meets the needs of all three of these groups.

You need to convey the basic idea about your company, and ideally tell some story about what makes your product or service unique.

This means that you'll need some content in very large type that is easy to read from 30 feet away, along with attractive images and colors. You'll also want more information that people can view for themselves; they may not want to engage with your staff but still want to get more details.

Finally, you want your booth to be inviting. A barrier of tables along the front of the booth does not encourage interaction. Instead, you want a space that visitors can step into and then engage with your staff. By getting them to "vote with their feet" and make that physical move to enter your space, you help encourage a conversation about your company. Note that this also means you need to have staff who are smiling, making eye contact with visitors, and are ready to engage them.

What About Giveaways?

Almost everyone loves free stuff, and people expect to see all sorts of handouts at trade shows. CES is certainly no exception. These can be a good way to garner goodwill and to help get your company name out into the hands of others.

They can also be a colossal waste of money.

For example, there must be hundreds of thousands of imprinted ballpoint pens manufactured each year just for CES exhibitors. And we suspect that the majority of these pens end up getting shipped home again (or thrown out).

People don't value pens, and they don't pay attention to the brand on them.

A bowl of candy (individually wrapped items) can be a popular feature, but it often goes to "drive-by" visitors who will grab a piece as they stroll by.

Good giveaways need to be valued by the visitor, either for the information it contains or for its utility. T-shirts are useful and remain a popular item, but few companies can afford to hand out thousands of them to visitors who are not qualified prospects.

If you do create gifts for visitors, make sure they are suitable for your brand and your product. For example, Livall is a company based in Shenzhen, China, that makes smart helmets for bicycling enthusiasts. According to Qi Wang, the company's PR & Project Management Director, the company had success with a giveaway item that was surprising and cool, and was useful for its target audience. It created riding gloves and riding apparel that had its logo on them. These turned out to be great at starting conversations, leading to deeper engagement with prospects.

Some exhibitors put their company information on a USB drive. These can be very effective, but they're a bit expensive to hand out to every passerby.

As a result, you may want to make only a limited number of items to give away to visitors, and then use them sparingly as a thank-you gift for those who come into your booth and engage in a conversation.

Booth Logistics

Be careful to consider all the implications of your design choices.

For example, how are you going to get the components to the exhibit hall? Will the pieces fold up and knock down in order to be small enough that you can ship them at a price that you can afford?

You also need to study the exhibit rules and provisions carefully, and if you have any questions, contact the CTA representatives early in the process so there are no surprises or misunderstandings.

For example, typically, you are limited to whatever you can carry by hand into the hall. If something needs to come in on a hand truck or dolly, then it will have to be handled by the exhibition services. Also be aware of the rules about what you are and are not permitted to do when it comes to assembling your booth displays. Even though you are quite capable of handling some tasks on your own, you may be required to pay for services to do these tasks for you.

You need to get all your materials to the hall early enough that there will be time for the exhibit services to get them to your booth space. And be sure to allow extra for the inevitable delays and other complications.

This means that you will need to get all these items designed and made well in advance. This is an essential part of your planning process; it will do you no good to go to the expense of launching a CES campaign if your materials aren't there in the booth when the lights go up.

Booth design is another area where it can make sense to outsource some or all of the decisions and preparation. If you don't have a lot of trade show experience, working with a company that can help design and execute your booth can be a very smart investment. If they have experience working with CES, it's even better, as they will be more likely to know where the pitfalls are hidden, and can help you avoid unpleasant and costly surprises.

Action Guide: Planning Your Booth

Here are some of the important points to consider about your booth exhibit at CES:

☐ Where do you want your booth to be located?

☐ How big a booth do you want?

☐ Who do you want to attract to your booth?

☐ What is the main story that you want to tell visitors?

☐ What signage will you have?

☐ What furniture and displays will you have?

☐ How many staff will you need to have in the booth at one time?

☐ What colors will you use for your booth and display?

STAN PICKS THE WRONG CES ALTERNATIVE EVENT

No, sorry ...
GPS units are
at Booth #72

BOOTH 71

Blazek

Chapter 5:
The Un-Booth –
Alternatives to Booth Exhibits

What if you don't have a budget big enough for even the smallest booth tucked away in the hinterlands of the CES exhibit spaces?

Or what if you want to increase your exposure, and maybe get more people interested in coming by your booth, if you do have one?

Consider the "un-booth." You have many alternatives to consider, some of which may be more effective than others.

Guerilla Marketing

One bright idea that startups seem to discover year after year is to skip getting a booth, and just get a crew of employees dressed in attention-getting outfits to roam the exhibit halls and show their product.

Sadly, it doesn't work all that well. As one entrepreneur described the experience, you quickly discover that nobody is going to notice you. It's nearly impossible to cut through the noise and bustle of the show.

How many of the 170,000 other attendees will you walk past? And even if this is a significant number, how can you hope that a significant portion of these will be the right people that you want to reach? And if you get in front of the right people, how many will you be able to engage effectively?

As tempting as street marketing may seem, it's been shown over and over again that it's not a very effective way to get attention and coverage at CES.

Fortunately, there are many viable alternatives to consider.

Press-Only Events

If your main goal is to reach the media, then you want to go where they are. There are a number of events held at CES, and you don't even have to be an exhibitor at the show in order to participate.

All of these events follow the same basic format. All the

exhibitors get a simple 6-foot or 10-foot table space (though you can get multiple tables if you need more room). Members of the press are invited to attend, with the added enticement of free food and beverages. These events run in the evening, when exhibit halls are closed. Compared with even the smallest booth exhibit, the total cost of participation can be much smaller.

These events have several advantages. Since they are only open to the media, you can focus on them without having to worry about doing deals with distributors or retailers, or having your space occupied by tire-kickers. The whole event fits in one large ballroom, so it is possible for a reporter to find all the relevant exhibitors during the course of the evening. And it's a level playing field; a major corporate exhibitor's table display is not going to look a whole lot different than that of a tiny startup. You've got an equal shot at getting attention.

There are three main press-only exhibit events at CES every year: CES Unveiled, Digital Experience, and ShowStoppers.

One of the most important points about these three activities is that they are not limited to just CES in Las Vegas. All three have versions held on multiple occasions throughout the year, and at venues around the world. The CTA holds CES Unveiled in New York, Paris, and Prague. The others have events at major conferences worldwide throughout the year. While we focus on the CES Las Vegas events here – either as a substitute or an adjunct to a CES exhibit booth – keep these in mind as a practical alternative or first step in your exhibition plans.

CES Unveiled: This event is held the night before the CES show starts in earnest. It comes at the end of the Press Day, where the media can attend press conferences offered by many of the major consumer electronics companies.

While CES Unveiled is part of the official CES activities and is run by the CTA, you do not have to be an exhibitor in the show to get a space at CES Unveiled. This can give you exposure to the press at a much lower cost.

The fact that it is held the night before the exhibit halls open means that you can get a jump on the media coverage. Part of WiseWear's success at creating a national buzz for its smart jewelry was the direct result of CES Unveiled. It was interviewed by a reporter from the technology news site Engadget, and the story was posted online just 30 minutes later. This early coverage was seen by others in the press corps, and the company ended up getting a steady stream of reporters through its booth all week.

Digital Experience: This show is completely independent of CES and is run by Pepcom. The company hosts similar events around the world throughout the year at other major conferences, including Mobile World Conference in Barcelona, Spain.

ShowStoppers: This is also an independent event, run by ShowStoppers. This group also hosts events year-round at conferences around the world, including IFA and NAB.

Many companies will exhibit at all three of these events, maximizing their exposure to the press. If media coverage is your primary goal, then these events may be the most leveraged opportunities for your CES investment.

Industry-Focused Events

A new type of CES activity has grown more popular in recent years. Industry groups and organizers have put together their own mini-trade shows and press events, focused on a specific area. Often, these are for the press and by invitation only, but some are open to other participants as well.

For example, the Bluetooth SIG (Special Interest Group) is an industry organization that exists to promote wireless Bluetooth technology. One way they do this is to hold media events throughout the year, including at CES. Member companies can participate at no extra cost, and demonstrate their products to members of the press. At CES 2016, 25 member companies participated, and more than 400 members of the media attended the event. Those are pretty good numbers if you're looking for exposure with the publications that cover your product area.

As you might imagine, a major event in Las Vegas is not going to be all business, all the time. The week is filled with parties, receptions, and other events for press, participants, and exhibitors. You have many opportunities to be a part of these events, from sponsorships to being able to demonstrate your products or services.

If you're part of an industry group or association, check to see if it has any events planned for CES and find out if there are ways you can participate. Also, search online for lists of CES parties and receptions, and see if any are targeted at your market. These can provide some affordable alternatives or additions to exhibit space in the CES convention halls.

Take the Stage

Whether you exhibit or not, consider making a presentation or speaking on a panel as part of the CES conference program. Many people don't realize that, while all those exhibit halls are filled with people visiting booths, there are also hundreds and hundreds of visitors attending the various conference sessions. More than 1,200 speakers – including C-level executives from major companies – present in the conference portion of the CES event.

Dr. Shai Gozani, CEO and President of NeuroMetrix, spoke on a panel that discussed the path to FDA clearance for software apps and health-related products. He credited the appearance with increased press attention for his company and its product.

You can propose to organize your own presentation. In addition to individual presentations, the conference includes panels where representatives from several companies in related industries get to share insider insights with the audience.

The CTA publishes information on the CES Call for Speakers page. This lists the many themes that the conference will focus on in the coming show. Note that the deadline for entering a speaker application is the middle of June in the prior year (in other words, slightly more than six months in advance), so you need to make your plans early.

There are also a number of "conferences within the conference" that are managed by different organizations. These events often include panel discussions, and you may be able to get onto a program related to your industry. Find out about these events and contact the organizers to offer to serve on a panel.

These can be very effective ways to get visibility and establish credibility. One company executive told us that his participation on an industry panel resulted in significant traffic to the company's booth during the show.

There are also "pay to play" events such as the popular "Last Gadget Standing" and "Mobile Apps Showdown" contests, where finalists demonstrate their products and a live audience chooses the winner on the spot. These events come with a lot of advance publicity, and companies that are finalists can get a lot of extra press coverage.

Find a Big Friend

One other strategy to reduce the costs of exhibiting at CES while increasing your exposure is to find a big friend who will let you tag along.

If your business relies on a specific component or technology, find out if the company behind that part of the puzzle will be exhibiting. It might like to include your company in its exhibit to provide a living case study about how it supports customers who rely on its products. If its product is particularly obscure or technical, having an end-user product on display can help make its product seem more relevant and useful.

You'll see examples of this at some of the biggest exhibits at the show. Major corporations such as Intel or Microsoft will have a village of little kiosks as part of their booth. Each kiosk will be staffed by a different company, showing off its products that are based on the host company's technology.

Not only does this result in much lower exhibit costs, it also lets you bask in the publicity glow of the larger corporation. People are more likely to come to the well-known company's booth, and can then discover your product when they get there.

You don't need to find an enormous company with which to make this sort of an arrangement, either. You may be able to share booth space with a much smaller company. (Note that CES has rules about booth sharing arrangements, so you'll want to check these out.)

The point is that if you have a close relationship with one of your suppliers – especially if it has invested in your company – you may be able to piggyback off its exhibit arrangements. As part of your planning process, contact key players in your supply chain and see if there is an opportunity for you to share their exhibit space at CES.

Keep Your Distance

There's one more important option to consider: a hospitality suite. If you don't need to be found, but instead want a quiet and comfortable place to meet with the press, potential investors, or prospective distributors or retailers, a room in a hotel may work best for you. You can get a suite with bedrooms, so that your accommodations and your exhibit space are the same place. And you can provide your own refreshments rather than pay catering prices for food and drink.

You're not limited to the exhibit hall hours, so you can

schedule meetings as early or as late as you wish. Depending on the amount of space you book, you can arrange for enough room to hold several meetings at one time. You can even have a "public" space where you have your products on display, and a "private" space where you can share confidential information such as a peek at pre-release prototypes or financial details.

This is a strategy that is used effectively by many companies. One year, the display company Kopin used a private suite to demonstrate new battery technologies and a noise-canceling technology that gathered international press coverage.

If you get space in a hotel on the same floor as other companies involved in the same market as yours, you can put a banner on a stand or an easel board announcing your presence to attract drop-in visitors who may have come to meet with your competitors.

For the most part, however, you'll only want to take this route if you are going to rely primarily on scheduled meetings with key contacts. You will have to identify these people well in advance, and do your best to get them to commit to a specific meeting time.

The big drawback with this strategy, however, is that it will take your visitors away from the convention center. Some people – especially members of the press – may be reluctant to take the time to travel away from the conference site, especially when the exhibit halls are open.

If you have a suite at the Westgate Las Vegas or the Renaissance Las Vegas, this may not be as much of a problem.

Both of these hotels are within relatively short walking distance from the Convention Center. It can take about the same amount of time to walk to the Westgate from the North Hall of the Las Vegas Convention Center (LVCC) as it takes to walk from the North Hall to the South Hall.

If you pick a more distant location, however, such as the MGM Grand or Mandalay Bay, then you could be asking someone to give up two hours or more just in order to have a 30 minute off-site meeting. That can be a tough sell.

Plenty of Options

The bottom line is that while you can go big with a splashy booth in the exhibit halls, you have other choices that could make your CES budget go further. Consider your options carefully; depending on your goals, you may find that a mix of two or more approaches will get you where you want to go.

Action Guide: Alternatives to a Booth

If your primary goal is media exposure, get details on these three major press-only events at CES:

☐ CES Unveiled

☐ Digital Experience

☐ ShowStoppers

Does your company belong to any industry groups or associations? If so, contact them and see if they will have any of the following activities at CES that you may be able to join:

☐ Press-only exhibit event

☐ Industry representative exhibit event

☐ Industry reception or party

☐ CES booth exhibit

Contact any companies in your supply chain to see if they have any of the following activities that you may be able to join:

☐ Press-only exhibit event

☐ Industry representative exhibit event

☐ Industry reception or party

☐ CES booth exhibit

Yeah, yeah, yeah ... I'll be at the booth soon. I can't leave until I get three Conditioners.

Blazek

Chapter 6:
Las Vegas Survivor Secrets

Las Vegas is a budget buster. No matter how much money or time you plan on spending, figure that you'll spend more than that. And sometimes, a lot more! A little preparation goes a long, long way to save you time and money as you try to survive CES in Las Vegas.

Getting Around Town

Let's start with the big one: how to get around town. And the big tip is that if you don't have to drive, don't. Parking is expensive and traffic can be a nightmare.

If you need to bring stuff for your booth, there are special arrangements for exhibitors who deliver their booth materials in a POV (Personally Owned Vehicle), but you'll want to read the rules and limitations carefully if you plan to go this route. (Remember, you can't cart your gear into the exhibit hall on your own. You're limited to what you can carry.) But it may work out better to simply have the materials shipped to the site so you don't have to worry about delivering them yourself.

If you're not going to drive, then how will you get around? To start with, forget taxicabs. Once the show starts, you can wait for hours to get a cab. There will be hundreds of people ahead of you in line. You should just go straight to Plan B without even considering taxis.

What about Uber? The service is now available in Las Vegas, but the pickup points are blocks from the Convention Center so you'll have to do some walking to get there. If you're leaving from some less-crowded location, such as a restaurant, Uber may be a viable option but be careful to check availability and fares before you commit.

During the show week when the exhibit halls are open, the CES shuttle service runs a pretty comprehensive set of routes that hit many of the major casino hotels. So long as you have your badge, you can ride these for free even if you're not staying in that particular hotel. If you're staying someplace nearby, you can just walk over and take the shuttle, which can save time and hassle. Plus, you get the opportunity to strike up conversations with others from the show; we've known of some significant deals and connections that were made during these shuttle bus rides.

At times, you may find that you have to travel from one casino or other major location to another. First-time visitors often look around and decide that their destination "doesn't look that far." Don't be deceived.

The fact is that Las Vegas buildings are built on a scale that is not familiar to most people. They are huge and there tends to be a lot of space between them. A single hotel/casino complex can easily span the equivalent of several blocks in a normal city.

If you're on the sidewalk looking down the Strip and you can see your intended destination, you may be tempted to try to just walk there. Chances are good that it will turn out to be a lot farther than you think.

Public Transportation

Fortunately, Las Vegas has an excellent public transportation system. The Regional Transportation Commission (RTC) has a network of buses that makes travel easy. It also offers a smartphone app called Ride Tracker that helps you plan your trip, and can even tell you when the next bus will arrive at a given stop.

Traveling the Strip is easy, using the Deuce and the Strip & Downtown Express routes. You can purchase tickets from vending kiosks at many bus stops; convenient all-day and multi-day passes let you ride any bus. At the time of publication, a 3-day pass cost just $20.

Note that RTC buses also provide service to and from

McCarran Airport. A short connecting bus ride will take you to a terminal where you can take the Strip & Downtown Express. If you want to save transportation costs and the CES shuttles aren't going where you need to go, the bus services make an affordable and convenient alternative.

The Monorail

The Las Vegas Monorail deserves separate mention. It is run by a private, nonprofit corporation, and receives no public funding. It was created to provide fast transportation between several of the major casinos on the Strip.

The trains run from MGM at the south end to the SLS Las Vegas (formerly the Sahara) at the north end. Stops along the way include one for the LVCC and one for the Westgate Las Vegas.

You can get single-ride tickets or multi-day passes, and you can even purchase them online. If the monorail goes where you need to go, it can be one of your best choices as it travels above the streets where traffic congestion can be a serious problem, especially when the CES exhibit halls are just opening or closing.

One big caveat about the monorail is that the stops are located at many of the major casinos, but they are often placed at a significant distance from the meeting areas or hotel rooms. You may have a significant walk ahead of you even once you reach the monorail stop, so be sure to allow for plenty of time to reach your final destination.

Finally, here's a big tip about using the monorail. The lines to get on the trains can get very long at the end of each day. If you don't want to wait in line, especially if you're located in the North Hall, it's worth the time to walk up to the monorail stop at the Westgate and get on there. Since this is only the second stop southbound, there will be far fewer people on the train at that point and you will have a good chance of getting on board without any wait at all. Just be prepared for a crush of people boarding when you get to the Convention Center stop, which is next along the line.

A Place to Stay

If you start early, you can find a hotel room with little trouble. If you wait until the last minute, prices may be high and the selection limited. You might even have to stay a considerable distance from the LVCC, which can add to your transportation costs, travel time, and frustration.

If you're bringing a team of employees, consider renting a house for the week. Online sites such as VRBO and FlipKey have homes and condos available for short-term rentals, including properties within walking distance of the LVCC. These can include parking – which can eliminate a major headache and expense if you're driving your own car – and other amenities such as a swimming pool. Best of all, a four-bedroom home that "sleeps 12" can be rented for less per night than just one room at a hotel on the Strip.

Renting your own place also means that you can provide your own food and prepare your own meals. This alone can save you hundreds of dollars a day, depending on the size of your team. We spoke with Dr. Gerald Wilmink, CEO of WiseWear, about this strategy. Not only did the company rent a house for its staff, but it even hired a part-time housekeeper to help with meals and managing the house.

Obviously, only a limited number of such properties are available, so it pays to book as far in advance as you can. It can be a great way to save money and provide a team-building experience for your employees as well.

Food and Drink

The one word of advice that we heard from just about everyone we interviewed for this project was "hydrate."

If you're not accustomed to the desert air, you may be surprised how quickly you can get dehydrated, even within the air-conditioned comfort of the exhibit halls and hotel rooms.

You also may not be attuned to some of the symptoms that go along with dehydration. These can often start long before you notice that you're thirsty. The chapped lips are one common sign, but so are fatigue and headache. In extreme cases, you may even get a nosebleed.

By the time you notice any of these symptoms, you will likely be significantly dehydrated and it will take plenty of water – and time – to reverse it. As a result, make sure that you and everyone on your team is proactive about drinking plenty of water throughout the day. Bring a case of bottled water to the booth every day, or better yet, equip your team with multiple refillable water bottles to save money. And then make sure that everyone keeps up their water consumption.

Here are two dangers to watch out for when it comes to dehydration. People often treat the symptoms, thinking that they're addressing the problem. As a result, some people will become fanatical about applying lip balm to prevent chapped lips. This will certainly help prevent their lips from drying out, but it does not address the root cause. It's fine to use lip balm if you want, but make sure you also drink lots of water.

In a similar vein, some people keep a bottle of water handy at all times, and take sips from it frequently. This helps keep their mouths from getting dry – especially when they're doing lots of talking – but again, it can mask the symptoms of dehydration. You can sip water all day and still end up significantly dehydrated. Take sips if you want, but still make sure that you drink lots of water as well.

If you're well hydrated, you still can run out of gas, so you'll want to have some good snacks on hand for the team. This will save lots of money because exhibit hall concessions (and hotel room service) are not known for their great prices. It will also save time because your team won't have to spend time waiting in long lines.

One important point about food at the show: Don't have your team members eat while in the booth. It makes them look disinterested or unapproachable, and can drive away traffic. One company executive told us that it is important to have your staff take their food to a seating area somewhere else in the hall when it's time to eat. Besides, this gives them a break and a chance to relax before returning to the booth.

Take the time to work with your team ahead of time to plan out snacks and other food preferences so that you have everyone covered. This will save you lots of time and energy once the show starts.

Sound Bodies

Exhibiting at a trade show is grueling work. There may be times when your booth is swamped with visitors requiring all hands on deck, which means people may have to miss a scheduled break.

On the other hand, you can go hours without a visitor, which makes it difficult to keep up your energy and enthusiasm when someone does appear.

You need to be prepared mentally and physically for this challenge. To start with, you'll want to be well rested and focused before you start, as you will tap your reserves sooner than you might think. While Las Vegas stays open 24/7, with an endless menu of entertainment options, make sure everyone gets a good night's sleep.

A word about alcohol: Drinking is closely associated with trade shows and with Las Vegas, so you are exposed to a double-whammy at CES. No doubt, product partners or retailers may want to wine and dine you, but play it smart. Alcohol can easily dehydrate you in the desert environment. But even more important is the fact that a hangover can undermine your energy and enthusiasm the following day. Your company is investing a lot of money and other resources to get exposure at CES. Don't blow it by over-indulging and ruining a day of hard-fought good work.

Also plan to be as comfortable as you can be during the show. How you choose to dress your team will be based on the type of image you want to project, but make sure it is a conscious decision rather than just leaving it to chance. Whether it's dress shirts and slacks or T-shirts and jeans, put some planning into what will show well and yet be comfortable for your team.

Remember that comfort starts at the bottom. You and your team will be on your feet most of each day, so make sure that you have several pairs of comfortable footwear available for the week. Even the best shoes can become a problem if you wear them every day without a break.

If you've got a booth space, you may want to consider paying more to get extra padding under the carpet. The hard concrete floor quickly takes its toll, and the more comfort you can provide, the more energy your team will have. You may also notice that visitors to your booth will relax a bit when they sense that softer footing; they've been on their feet all day, too.

Action Guide: Survivor Secrets

Write down the different types of transportation needs
that you anticipate during CES. Consider which modes of
transportation will be most cost-effective and time-efficient
for each one: your own car, a rental car, taxi, Uber, CES
shuttles, public buses, monorail, or other choices.

_____

_____

_____

_____

_____

Make a list of the pros and cons of different lodging options,
such as the larger hotel/casinos, motels, and rental condos
and houses. For each one, consider different factors including:

- ☐ Total cost
- ☐ Accommodations
- ☐ Amenities
- ☐ Location
- ☐ Convenience factors

What snacks and meals will work best for your team members?

_____

_____

_____

_____

_____

_____

FRANK GETS HELP WITH THE BOOTH

CES
EXHIBIT AREA
←

They're freelancers. Apparently it's their off-season or something.

Blazek

Chapter 7:
Go It Alone or Get Help?

Let's face it: There are a lot of moving parts to mounting a CES campaign. Each part requires different skills and knowledge, and all require time and money.

If your company is small – and even if it's not – the added burden of getting all these tasks accomplished on time, effectively, and at minimum cost can put a significant strain on the rest of your operations.

It's entirely possible that you don't even have the necessary talent and experience on staff to accomplish some of these tasks. One of the admirable traits of entrepreneurs with a startup company is that they have an indomitable "can do" attitude. There's no problem that can't be conquered by rolling up your sleeves and figuring out the solution on your own.

That's an admirable mind-set, but it can get you in trouble. Getting behind deadlines, the risk of wasting precious resources on an event, and the crush of extra work in desperate last-ditch efforts can have a corrosive effect on an organization. It can take a long time to recover from this damage, and it can be enough to sink a company.

There are times when it just makes sense to get help. One advantage of using outside services is that you get to rent the knowledge and skills that you need without committing to adding these to your staff permanently. You avoid increasing your overhead costs by turning to short-term solutions.

Services for Hire

As a result, it makes sense to consider getting some outside help as you build your CES campaign. Here are some of the different areas that might be worth investigating:

Graphic Design: Even if your company already has its logo and other branding elements firmly in place, hiring a graphic designer for some of your projects could be a good idea. From handouts to giveaways, you'll need designs that can grab the visitor's eye and convey your company's story as quickly and effectively as possible.

Booth Design: The creation of your booth (or table exhibit if you're planning on some of the press-only events) is a critical part of your campaign. Sure, you can throw something together on your own, but it is critical that you attract visitors to your booth.

You may want to go to an exhibit rental company that can help you with everything from soup to nuts, and even deliver you a turnkey solution if you want. Many firms have affordable packages that can be customized at a very reasonable cost, and their designers are skilled and experienced at creating trade show booths that are effective.

An added benefit of working with such a company is that it will have lots of experience with the logistic requirements at trade shows. You might even want to pick one that has experience specifically with CES. Rather than have to figure it out for yourself – and run the risk of making a costly mistake – you can arrange it so that you can show up and find your booth all set up, waiting and ready for you to move in. And at the other end, it all gets boxed up for you and you don't have to worry about getting it shipped back out.

Public Relations: A good public relations firm can help with getting press coverage for your CES campaign. For example, they will know how to use inexpensive press releases most effectively to get your news in front of the right media representatives.

More important, however, is the fact that they already have the contacts that you need. If you can find a firm that already works with other companies within your same market segment, they should already know who the key reporters are for the major publications and news outlets. In many cases, the agents already have a direct relationship with these people, with an established trust that helps them deliver their clients' messages with greater success.

These same contacts and relationships can increase your chances of making booth appointments with key media. You can even arrange to have one or more of the agency staff join your team to be on hand solely for the press. This means that you'll have a skilled and experienced person ready to field questions and help put reporters together with the right person on your team as needed.

Marketing: A good marketing service can help you hone your company's message. Many small companies are started by people with excellent technical and entrepreneurial skills, but they may not be the best at explaining their product or service.

A good marketing firm can help you create a unified, cohesive message about your company, and can help develop strategies to get that message in front of your target market. They can help with everything from strategic planning to writing copy for your promotional materials.

Again, it helps to work with a firm that already has experience working with other companies within your same general industry as they are more likely to understand some of the pivotal issues for your customers.

Finding the Right Service

When you rely on an outside service, you are trading your company's money to save your staff's time. You will want to get the best value possible in return for your investment.

As with finding any resource, one of the most powerful sources of information is your own network of contacts. Ask around to find people and services that are recommended. A personal referral can often be the best way to find help.

Don't forget to include contacts in your industry associations or in online groups that focus on your industry. These can be excellent sources of references.

When picking a service, be sure to find out about their experience. If you can work with people who have helped with CES campaigns in the past, they are more likely to know about the hidden pitfalls and mistakes to avoid. You may as well get experience at the same time that you're paying for skill.

Also, look for companies that can provide as many of the services that you need as possible. They may have the necessary resources in-house, or they may be able to provide some through the use of sub-contractors. This approach gives you a single point of contact for all your support, and decreases the chances that you'll have your support companies working at cross-purposes with each other.

Outside services can be a real multiplier for your own staff's productivity. By farming out the pieces that can be handed off, your people will be able to focus on the parts that need their specific attention, and will give them more time to get their "regular" work done.

Action Guide: Outside Help for Your Campaign

Consider the in-house resources you have and their availability for extra work to prepare for a CES campaign. Score each one from 1 to 5 where 1 is "We can do it all" and 5 is "We need someone to do it all."

Score	1	2	3	4	5
Graphics	☐	☐	☐	☐	☐
Booth design/rental	☐	☐	☐	☐	☐
Public relations	☐	☐	☐	☐	☐
Marketing	☐	☐	☐	☐	☐

What task is the top priority for getting outside help?

_____

_____

_____

_____

What task is the second priority for getting outside help?

_____

_____

_____

_____

_____

Chapter 8:
Make the Most of
Your Investment

"What happens in Las Vegas stays in Las Vegas."

That may be a fine sentiment for a bachelor party, but when it comes to a major international trade show like CES, that's a recipe for disaster. After spending a week with more than 170,000 potential new friends, you want to make sure that you do not waste a single bit of the time and money you invested in making your campaign a success.

And that means following the leads.

Plan the Work

Like so many aspects of success at CES, you need to plan how you will handle the information you get from visitors at the show. The more you can figure out in advance, the easier it will be to get the best return on your investment.

Have you ever returned from a conference or a meeting with a pile of business cards, and little or no idea what you're supposed to do with each one? Which ones require a follow-up contact? Which ones requested something in particular from you? And which ones were totally unqualified and you only took their cards to be polite?

If you're going to be spending tens of thousands of dollars and weeks (or months) of combined staff time on this project, you don't want to have just a pile of random business cards to show for your efforts.

Make lead acquisition a primary part of your planning. There are several aspects that you need to consider.

For example, how will you capture visitor information? Will you use the show's service to scan badges? This costs extra, but it means that you get contact information in digital format. You won't have to invest additional time scanning or typing the information into a contact database. Plan on spending from $275 for a single license for a smartphone app, to $500 for a rented tablet. (These are the discounted online rates; you'll pay 20% to 40% more if you order later.)

On the other hand, it may cost less to pay a typist to enter data from business cards, or scan them using a scanner.

In either case, you'll need to have a system that allows you to segment the contacts. You'll need to know which ones are members of the press, or distributors, or retailers, or investors, or suppliers, or something else. Some of our press contacts tell us that one of the most annoying aspects of CES is that they inevitably get called by at least one company trying to sell their product or service. Members of the press are not potential customers, and it's a waste of their time and yours to pester them to try and make a sale.

You also will need to track which contacts need a specific response. Perhaps it's a distributor who wants a sample to inspect, or maybe a reporter needs some technical information that is not available on your website. Make sure that you have a system that will capture these requests, and track the deadlines for each one.

The third part of your lead planning is to assign the responsibility for various tasks to your team members. Is everyone going to be responsible for everything, or are only certain people going to speak with visitors from certain segments? Who gets to talk with distributors and retailers, and should that be a different person from the staff who will deal with reporters and other members of the media?

Make sure the system covers as many contingencies as possible. If you're planning to mark business cards with a note or symbol to categorize them, know what you'll do when confronted with one with a black background, or a coating that won't take ink from a pen. And if you're taking notes on a separate form, how will you keep the business card information with it? Some cards resist stapling, or come in unusual form factors. Be ready for anything.

Finally, make sure that everyone involved understands how the system is supposed to work, and what their role in the process will be. If possible, do some practice runs to make sure that you have all the bases covered. You don't want to be working out the kinks on the fly when you're standing in a crowded booth at the show.

Work the Plan

If your planning is thorough, you'll be ready to capture contact information efficiently and reliably right from the start of the show.

Remember that the contact information is the gold that you're trying to mine at the show, so treat it as the valuable asset that it is. Make sure that it is secure in your booth, and any forms or business cards or other notes are stored in a location where they won't get lost or mixed in with other materials.

Secure the information every night, and if at all possible, make a backup in case something happens to it. This could be as simple as using your smartphone to take photos of every business card. The added benefit is that most phones now also upload the images to cloud storage, so you have yet another copy of the data, just in case. Or you can bring a portable scanner on the trip, and scan business cards into a database on your laptop computer.

After the Deluge

With any luck, you and your team will come back with a

small mountain of new contacts and leads. Maybe even a large mountain. And the more you have already planned how to handle this, the better off you'll be.

Keep in mind that this can swamp your existing lead-management process. If you were handling two to 10 contacts a day under normal circumstances, you could find yourself in the situation where you need to deal with hundreds of leads in a very short window. Plan in advance how you're going to assign your resources – or bring in extra temporary help – to handle the follow-up without the rest of your business operations grinding to a complete halt.

Your efforts to segment the contacts and track any special responses will pay off handsomely at this point. You will be able to give the right leads to the right people. Sales staff can handle the sales calls, technical people can handle the technical questions, and the right management people can field opportunities with potential suppliers, partners, and investors.

In general, put the people who have specific requests at the top of the queue. Everyone will be digging out from all their backlog the week after CES, but you want to respond to specific requests as quickly as possible.

This is especially true for members of the media. If they are interested enough in your product to request spec sheets, product photos, or other materials, they are more likely to write about it.

Note that for many media outlets these days, stories have an incredibly short shelf life. Some editors won't take stories that are more than twenty-four hours old, so it pays to know who your press contacts write for and their requirements for a "good" story. For those on tight deadlines, you'll want to fill their request that same night from your hotel room, if not sooner.

For the general follow-ups, the timing will vary from one segment to another. For example, you'll probably have the most success with the press if you check in with them between Wednesday and Friday the week after the show. Unless you have a compelling reason to do otherwise, follow up with the press by email. Most reporters view unsolicited and unscheduled phone calls as an unwanted interruption.

For others, follow your usual protocols, using email or phone calls or a combination as needed. You've got fertile fields to plow for new customers or partners, so give them a couple days to recover from the show and then make it clear that you want to continue the conversation that you started in Las Vegas.

Be Patient

Is your investment in CES worth it? You need to track the outcomes and keep a tally of the business that comes about as a result, but remember to take the long view.

Keep in mind that conversations with prospects can take a long time to bear fruit. We spoke with one executive who was excited to report that his company had just closed a deal to have its product carried in the Target retail store chain. This deal was the result of meeting a buyer from the retail giant at CES … the previous year! It took more than 15 months to complete the deal.

Action Guide: Make the Most of Follow-Up

What are the main segments of visitors that you will want to track at the show?

_____

_____

_____

_____

_____

Which members of your team will be responsible for collecting contact information and follow-up requests?

_____

_____

_____

_____

_____

Will you have enough employee bandwidth to handle all the follow-up tasks required the week after the show? Will you need to bring in extra resources to help make contacts?

_____

_____

_____

_____

_____

Summary:
Lather, Rinse, Repeat

As they turn off the lights in the empty exhibit halls and you make your way back home, the next CES may be the last thing on your mind. But keep in mind that it is already less than a year away.

In fact, you'll probably start thinking about the next CES while the show is in full swing. One reason for this is that current exhibitors get first pick on booth space reservations for the following year. You will have incentives to decide whether or not you're going to return.

Repeat Benefits

It is probably apocryphal, but do you know the one word that doubled shampoo sales? That word is "repeat," as in "lather, rinse, repeat." By getting customers to do the process twice, the shampoo companies doubled the consumption rate.

The fact is that repeating your CES campaign has a number of significant benefits to consider.

First, almost nobody hits a grand slam the first time at bat, and you will no doubt have a list of ideas and suggestions about how you could do things differently and better the next time. Some small changes can bring a big boost to your returns.

Also, you will have experienced the mayhem that is CES and survived. Whether you successfully avoided all the pitfalls, or perhaps fell into one or two along the way, you will have a much better idea about what it takes to have things run smoothly.

You will also have had ample opportunity to observe what your neighbors in the exhibit hall did that seemed to work well for them, or perhaps not so well. You will be able to incorporate these in your lessons learned from the week.

On the Record

If you can find the time, consider keeping a journal during the show where you can record your observations and ideas from the week. It can be in your phone or tablet, or in a small paper notebook that you keep in a back pocket. Or maybe you'll wait until the evening to write down as much as you can remember, though this can be less effective.

You may want to enlist some or all of your team to keep a similar record of what works and doesn't work. In addition to building a sense of shared purpose and camaraderie, you may get a treasure trove of good ideas that can save money or increase your next campaign's effectiveness.

It can also be helpful to do a debrief soon after the show ends, either as a group or individually. For example, a team dinner after the show closes can be a great opportunity to share ideas about what went well and what could be improved the next time.

By the time you do an evaluation of the follow-up efforts and compile the shared experience of the team members, you will be well on your way to planning your next campaign. You'll find it a lot easier the second time around, because it will be more familiar and you'll know better what to expect.

Action Guide: Planning for Next Year

Consider keeping a journal during the show, and having some or all of your team keep their own journal. It can serve as a record of the following:

☐ Items that worked well

☐ Items that didn't work as well

☐ Items about neighboring exhibits that worked

☐ Items about neighboring exhibits that did not work

☐ Pitfalls to avoid if at all possible

☐ New ideas to try next year

Have a group or individual debriefing for the team right after the show. What suggestions and ideas for the next year have the greatest potential?

_____

_____

_____

_____

_____

About the Authors

Mike Lizun is Senior Vice President with Gregory FCA with more than 18 years of experience in public relations, journalism, and communications. He has developed relationships with hundreds of contacts at the top-tier media companies covering technology, consumer, and business beats, including AP, Reuters, The Wall Street Journal, The New York Times, Fortune, TechCrunch, Good Morning America, TODAY Show, USA Today, ABC News, CNN, Forbes, and Fox News. He is an expert at winning national and international coverage for his clients, and is skilled at using social media engagement tactics to promote content.

You can contact Mike at mike@gregoryfca.com or through his LinkedIn profile at http://www.linkedin.com/in/mikelizun.

Matt McLoughlin is a CES veteran and a Vice President at Gregory FCA. Matt has secured top-tier stories for everything from a single molecule to flexible displays, and all kinds of gadgets, software, and components in between. His extensive network of top-tier contacts work at some of the largest and most influential media outlets in the world, and he has placed clients in stories with TIME Magazine, CNN, CBS Evening News, Associated Press, USA Today, The Wall Street Journal, The New York Times, Bloomberg Businessweek, MSNBC, and The Washington Post. He manages a passionate and experienced team focused on the technology sector.

You can contact Matt at matt@gregoryfca.com or through his LinkedIn profile at https://www.linkedin.com/in/mcloughlinmatthew.

Alfred Poor, Ph.D., is an accomplished speaker and writer. He has written or co-authored more than a dozen books, and thousands of his articles, reviews, and commentary have been published in major magazines, including Businessweek and PC Magazine, and online for FOX News, Verizon, and Hewlett Packard, among others.

For more information about Alfred Poor and his services, you can find out more at his website at *www.alfredpoor.com*. You can also contact him by email at **alfred@alfredpoor.com** or by phone at **215-453-9312**.

Follow Mike on Twitter at **@MikeLizun**

Follow Matt on Twitter at **@mmclough**

Follow Alfred on Twitter at **@AlfredPoor**

About Gregory FCA

Whether you're advancing consumer tech in smart homes, wearables, or connected devices; mapping the future of car tech; engineering the future of robotics and drones; or pushing the limits of materials science, you're changing the world. Gregory FCA will make sure the world knows it.

Gregory FCA is a nationally ranked, full-service public relations firm that has spent the last 25 years helping companies tell their stories and drive new business through media relations, content marketing, social media, and event strategy. Gregory FCA's understanding of the technology and public relations landscape has propelled dozens of consumer technology companies into CES headlines over the past decade.

Find Gregory FCA online:

www.GregoryFCA.com

www.TheNewsHackers.com

www.Facebook.com/GregoryFCA

www.Twitter.com/GregoryFCA/

www.LinkedIn.com/company/Gregory-FCA

www.ingramcontent.com/pod-product-compliance
Lightning Source LLC
Chambersburg PA
CBHW071453200326
41519CB00019B/5721